Butterflies By

Hunter

Can you name this butterfly?
Come back after you read this
book and see if you can then.

This book is written by Hunter Riley Fugate age eight of Kettering, Ohio. Images courtesy of Bing free images and added by Hunter's grandmother Dee Lynn Jones.

Amazon Independent Publishing Platform

Seattle, Wa.

Library of Congress Control Number: 2015903146

Amazon Independent Publishing Platform, 4900 Lacross Rd, North Charleston, SC 29406

Title ID: 5071817

ISBN-13: 978-1502988423

Printed in the U.S.A.

This edition first printing, October, 2014

Prologue

Butterflies come in all shapes and sizes. Some even use camouflage to hide from predators. Above is a common Tiger Butterfly.

The Monarch Butterfly:

Monarch Butterflies have their bright colors to scare off predators. They also will poison any other animal that would eat them.

The Swallow Tail Butterfly:

These butterflies live mostly in tropical regions.
Members of this butterfly family inhabit every
continent except Antarctica. They are one of the
largest butterflies known.

The Glass Wing Butterfly:

This butterfly's tissue between the veins of its wings has no colored scales making it look like glass.

The Buckeye Butterfly:

This butterfly inhabits most of the United States except for the Pacific Northwest.

The Blue Morpho Butterfly:

These adult butterflies drink the juices of rotting fruits. When they are in caterpillar form they are a red-brown color with bright patches of lime green on their backs.

Metamorphosis:

There are four different stages to
Metamorphosis.

Metamorphosis:

Dozens of butterfly eggs hatching into larva.

Amazing!

Butterfly larva:

Notice the eye on the side and nose in the front?

The Monarch Caterpillar

Metamorphosis: The Monarch Butterfly is born

Awesome!

The American Snout Butterfly:

This butterfly has long labial palps (mustachelike
scaly mouthparts on either side of the proboscis)
that look like a long snout.

The Goliath Birdwing Butterfly:

This butterfly is the second largest in the world.
It will also poison its predators when eaten.

A Regular Birdwing Butterfly:

This butterfly is also very large in size and it comes
in various bright colors. It is my Grandma's favorit

The Julia Butterfly:

Linda Karlin 2008

These are found in South and Central America
and the southern United States. They have large
heads and smell bad.

The Ulysses Butterfly:

This bright blue and black Australian Swallow Tail lives in tropical rain forests. It can mostly be found around Australia and Indonesia and other nearby islands.

The Painted Lady Butterfly:

This may be the most widespread butterfly in the world. It can be found in North and South America as well as Europe, Asia and Africa.

The Southern Dog Face Butterfly:

This butterfly gets its name from the large dark circle in the wings and the margins are black like a dog's face.

Can you name these butterflies now? Go back
and look again if you are not sure.

Bonus Butterflies:

The Rainbow Butterfly:

One of the rarest of all butterflies lives in South America in a wetland forest.

The Purple Emperor Butterfly:

This rare butterfly lives in Europe.

The Red Spotted Purple Butterfly:

A species of North American butterfly,
common in much of the eastern United States.

The Red Admiral Butterfly:

This is a well-known colorful butterfly, found in temperate Europe, Asia and North America's warmer climates.

One last butterfly for you…

The extremely rare Red Monarch Butterfly.
Once in a while the tissues will be reddish
instead of their normal golden orange color.

Next, enjoy some photos of butterflies and a page from Hunter's notebook he made that started this book...

Southern Dogface

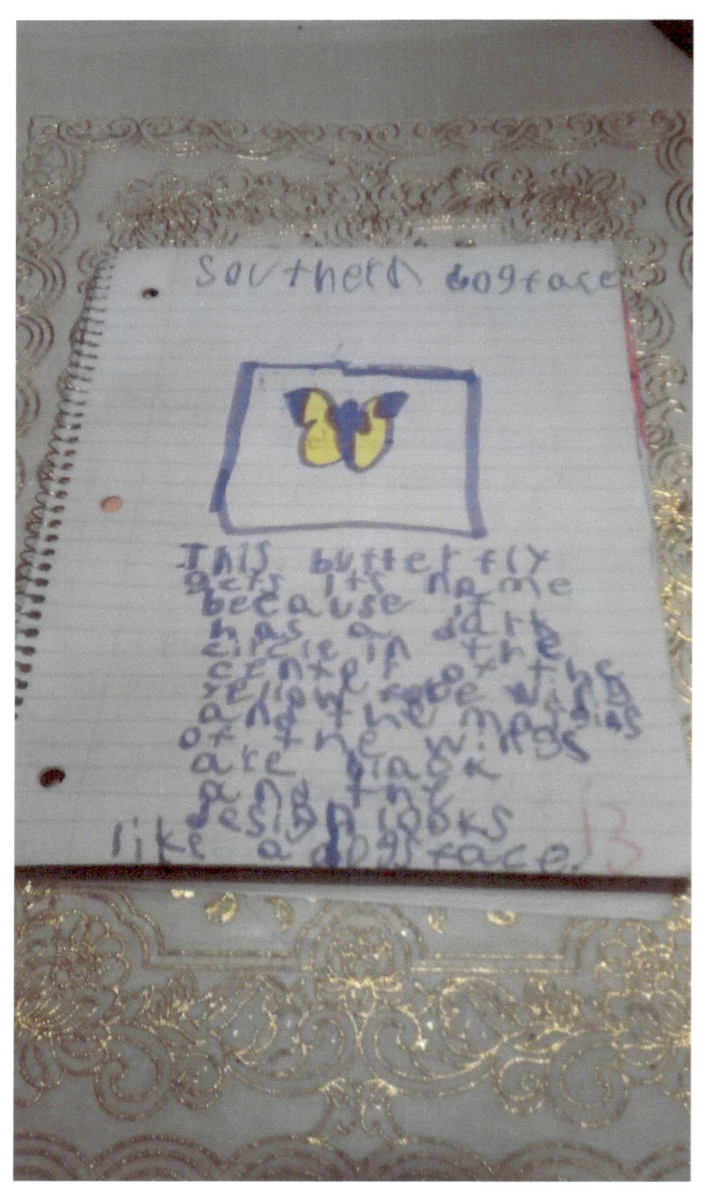

This butterfly gets its name because has a dark circle in the center of the yellow rear wings of the other wings are black and it looks like a dogface. 13

This page was one of many made by Hunter in his notebook he gave to his grandmother.

Reference page

Bing Royalty Free Images of Butterflies:

http://www.bing.com/images/search?q=butterf
ly&qs=IM&form=QBIR&pq=butterfly&sc=8-
9&sp=1&sk=

Also Wikipedia:

http://en.wikipedia.org/wiki/Butterfly

And Enchanted Learning

http://www.enchantedlearning.com/subjects/b
utterflies/allabout/